Running Your Tutor Group

Also available in the *Classmates* series:

Running Your Tutor Group

Ian Startup

continuum
LONDON • NEW YORK

Continuum

The Tower Building   15 East 26th Street
11 York Road   New York
London SE1 7NX   NY 10010

www.continuumbooks.com

British Library Cataloguing-in-Publication Data
A catalogue record for this book is available from the British Library.

ISBN 0-8264-6424-6

Typeset by BookEns Ltd, Royston, Herts.
Printed and bound in Great Britain by Biddles Ltd, Guildford and King's Lynn

Contents

Series Introduction

Dear Teacher

Classmates is an exciting and innovative new series developed by Continuum, and is designed to help you improve your teaching, and your career.

With your huge workload both inside and outside of school, we understand that you have less and less time to read around your profession. These short, pithy guides have been designed with an accessible layout so that you don't have to wade through lots of dull, heavy text to find the information you need.

All our authors have experienced teaching first hand and have written this essential series with busy teachers in mind. Our subjects range from taking school trips (*Tips for Trips*) and dealing with parents (*Involving Parents*) to coping with the large amounts of stress in your life (*Stress Busting*) and creating more personal time for yourself (*Every Minute Counts*).

If you have practical advice that you would like to share with your fellow teachers and think you could write a book for this series then we would be delighted to hear from you.

We do hope you enjoy reading our *Classmates*.
With very best wishes,

Continuum's Education Team

P.S. Watch out for our second batch of ten *Classmates*, to be launched in March 2004.

Introduction: What is the Role of the Tutor?

Imagine that on the day you arrive at your new school the head teacher comes up to you and says 'Oh, by the way, could you play the piano for us in assembly this morning?' You would know exactly what to say – 'I'd love to but I don't know how to play', 'I'm not at all musical', 'With some training I'd be happy to' and so on. What if instead the head turns to you and says 'Oh, by the way, could you take on a tutor group for us this morning?' Your response would be 'Which year group?', 'I'll just get my red pen' or 'No problem at all'.

Why is it that we can see that playing the piano is difficult unless we have trained and practised, and yet we think that managing a tutor group is something everyone can do? And yet, newly qualified teachers invariably admit that the most difficult and sometimes the most demoralizing aspect of starting a new job is working with a tutor group. Often they have received little or no training at college and teaching practise experience is limited.

The aim of this short book is to highlight some of the issues facing the new tutor and to suggest ways of developing the skills required to manage your tutor group. Certainly Ofsted regard the role of the tutor as important. In a recent report on a successful secondary school they said: 'Form tutors develop close, ongoing relationships with students and are very effectively involved in monitoring both academic performance and personal development.' By way of contrast, Ofsted inspectors observed of a failing school that 'little is done by the staff to define and secure a distinctive and appropriate school culture. For example, the form tutors make too little use of the time devoted to registration periods to induct pupils into their next session of lessons'. Furthermore, current concerns – the exclusion of students and increasing truancy rates – highlight the role of the tutor as a vital element of the educational process.

The role of the tutor in most schools is to take the register. This is not a highly demanding task and takes about five minutes (if you spin it out). Naturally there is more to it, but the mistake of many teachers is to think that this is all they have to do. In fact, the tutor is a key figure within the complex process of communication within the school. Messages from teachers to individual students, information about sports matches, room changes, etc., all pass through the tutor's hands. Keeping your tutor group informed about the day-to-day routines helps them feel part of what can sometimes feel like a very remote institution. The tutor is the distribution point for letters to parents, newsletters and other routine mail drops. The tutor plays a functional role in the routines of the school day. But none of these functions require a highly trained, well-paid graduate. Indeed, in the search for ways of reducing the workload of teachers some have pointed out that this aspect of a teacher's role could be given over to teaching assistants and electronic swipe cards. However, being a good tutor is not simply about administration: this is merely the easy bit.

More importantly, the tutor greets his or her students every morning, sets them up ready to learn for the rest of the day and starts the process of establishing the school ethos. It is the role of the tutor to establish school rules, monitoring uniform and behaviour. This is a frontline role. The tutor is often the first teacher to have to deal with problems. Tutors have to make quick judgement calls. Often, the tone they set with students makes the difference between an individual having a good day or going on to be disruptive. Many subject teachers feel that they waste time during the first lesson of the day because they have to spend time getting their class ready to learn. 'If only the tutor was doing their job properly', they say, 'we could get on with the work straight away.' And they are right. Time spent in a focused way will help your colleagues, and it will help your students as well.

Within some schools the tutor is responsible in part or wholly for the delivery of aspects of the curriculum, notably Personal, Social and Health Education and also Citizenship. In schools which follow this route for the delivery of key elements of the National Curriculum the tutor is a central part of a teaching team. While some might argue that this is undesirable, many tutors need to become experts on drugs, sex, relationships, the world of work and the making of citizens. Without relevant training tutors are often left feeling ineffective and exposed. And yet, the opportunity of teaching a diverse range of issues and ideas to a disparate group of children can be highly rewarding and a refreshing change from the normal classroom routines.

However, the tutor is not simply the instrument of the school. The role is more like a priest, a point for two-way communication between the students and the school. Often the tutor is the first to pick up problems in teaching groups: 'I hate maths!' followed by 'Mr Haynes can't teach!' is often a call for help. What the student is sometimes saying is 'My maths lesson is being disrupted by other students, the teacher is not coping, can you help?' Tutors feel that they must jump immediately to the defence of colleagues – 'I don't want to hear you talk about Mr Haynes like that!' is the end of the discussion. But the problem still remains. A response like 'What exactly is the problem?' infers no criticism of Mr Haynes but allows the student to define his or her concerns. Once the problem is defined it can then be dealt with effectively. Talking to the teacher concerned or raising the issue with the head of department can lead to resolution. 'I've had a word about that problem in maths, let me know if there is still a problem', neatly rounds off the situation. Often a parental letter of complaint, three months later, is averted by the tutor.

But whose side are you on? Do you ultimately take the side of the school or the student? In fact there is no real conflict of interests. The aim of all schools is to do the very best for their students. Therefore the tutor only has to answer one simple question: 'How can I help this student succeed in school?' But this does not always mean supporting the student come what may. There are times when what the student wants is not in their best interests: tutors, in a sense, must constantly make judgements about the best interests of the student.

Tutors sometimes view their role as akin to a social worker. This is a mistake, as tutors are rarely trained social workers or counsellors. However, tutors often become aware of issues relating to student welfare – from what they are told or from what they observe – that lead them to concerns. Here, the tutor's role is to identify problems and appropriate support mechanisms. The danger is that untrained meddling can make any problem worse.

Summary

- The role of the tutor is varied: schools will have different perceptions and expectations.

- The role of the tutor is not simply that of an administrator.

- The tutor can play a key role in establishing the school's ethos.

- The tutor can be instrumental in securing a positive learning experience for young people.

1

Registration and Keeping Records

As I have already indicated, I do not see administration as the prime function of a tutor. However, it is important. Registers can be used as evidence in a court of law. An accurate record is essential as more parents are taken to court for failing to keep their children in school and as crime rates increase amongst young people. Moreover, school finances are, in a sense, defined by the student roll; the register provides evidence required by auditors. Moreover, there is a clear and important link between student attendance and achievement. In a culture of target setting and improvement, therefore, maintaining and improving attendance is important. In all of this the tutor is at the front line, as the Audit Commission website recognizes:

Improving school attendance and behaviour in schools is vital if all children are to make the most of their educational opportunities. Its importance has been underlined by the government's decision to set targets for reducing levels of truancy and exclusions from school.
(Audit Commission, 2002)

In a letter to school governors in 1999 the DfES said:

We are working towards a simple but challenging goal: to raise educational standards for all our young people, who deserve the best possible chances in life. Regular attendance and high standards of pupil behaviour are vital to this goal. To help achieve it, we have set out to reduce the level of unauthorised absence and exclusions by one third by 2002.

It is interesting that the DfES made a clear link between standards of pupil behaviour and attendance. I'm not convinced that the link is inevitable but it certainly exists in the case of some students. Sometimes, helping to resolve inappropriate behaviour will resolve attendance problems (see Chapter 5, Managing difficult students). However, Mike Tomlinson, the Chief Inspector of Schools in England and Wales, commented in a report written in 2002:

It is worrying that, this year, there has been a slight decline in levels of attendance. Some schools have particular difficulties improving attendance levels when so many children have their absence condoned by parents. Over 80 per cent of young people stopped in shopping malls during school time by the police or welfare service are accompanied by an adult.

(Tomlinson, 2002)

It is not therefore necessarily just in school where problems of attendance are created, but also at home. However, it is far more difficult for a tutor to deal with this kind of problem. Absences that are always authorized by a note but do not seem justified or are simply too frequent to be convincing may be difficult to challenge. When the problem is rooted in family or social problems it is rarely possible for the tutor to establish the kind of relationship that will lead to a change in attitude. The best chance a tutor has of changing this situation is working with the student by developing a relationship based on mutual trust and respect.

It is important to first establish with the whole group why attendance is important. They need to know that their attainment in school will relate to their attendance levels. Talk to the group about a target for each student – say 95 per cent attendance in a half term. Work out with them how many sessions there will be in the period and how many they need to attend. This may, however, lead to some students assuming that they are entitled to take 5 per cent leave! This attitude can be tempered by explaining that there are absences that are unavoidable, through illness and so on, and that their full attendance will help to keep the group attendance averages high. All this seems mechanistic and does not fit with my overriding philosophy, which is rooted in creating relationships with your tutees. However, the two approaches are not exclusive; the setting of targets should not replace the creation of positive relationships. Equally, as tutor you do need to help your tutees maintain good levels of attendance as this will help them to ensure that they are more successful at school.

Within a culture that values attendance you can then deal with individual students. You need to establish opportunities within your room for confidential discussions – at your desk or by sitting next to the student. By talking, individually, about their reasons for absence you can foster a relationship that goes beyond the mechanistic calling of a register. It will help you to ensure that the absence is valid and will offer a context for discussing any patterns of absence and underlying anxieties. Linking attendance to attainment will help the student to understand your concern and may lead them to attend school more frequently.

Running Your Tutor Group

An Ofsted report on attendance in 2001 states that 'consistency in registration procedures and regular monitoring by senior managers are essential. Systematic follow-up of unexplained or inadequately excused absence is vital'. From this source it is clear that the function of the tutor in monitoring attendance is vital, not least because there is a direct correlation between attendance and attainment. While the tutor cannot act alone, and must rely on the systems in place within the school, it is vital that the tutor actually applies the systems – not because we want to hound children and parents, but because we want them to succeed within the existing educational structures.

Taking a register is undoubtedly a chore, and as there is increasing attention paid to teacher workload the likelihood is that electronic systems will replace the red pen. However, the taking of a register can help set the tone for the rest of the day. A chaotic registration will carry over into the next lesson. Always insist that the students are silent, and that they respond clearly. Some teachers successfully make a game of this. A number is allocated to each student who, at every registration, shouts out the number. The teacher notes the missing numbers and the task is done. Timing the process adds to the excitement! Once established as a routine it can run like clockwork. If you want to get clever you can get students to learn their numbers in a variety of different languages. It is fun to impress visitors to the class by conducting a quick-fire registration in Japanese or Swahili. Furthermore, this can be a part of building a group ethos.

Students are always keen to take the register, but keeping an accurate register is the responsibility of

'The taking of a register can help set the tone for the rest of the day. A chaotic registration will carry over into the next lesson' the teacher, so I think it is best to stick to the tutor as the one wielding the red pen. However, it is good to give responsibilities to students in the registration process. Reading out messages or collecting and returning the register are all ways of helping to establish a group identity (see Chapter 2). Later, in writing the tutor report, you can then comment on the student's reliability, helpfulness and so on. Every moment spent with the student is an opportunity for you to build up evidence of their ability to contribute in a productive way to the school and tutor group community, which in turn will make attendance at school a positive, rather than a chore.

Summary

- Student attendance is linked to student attainment.

- The register is a vital tool for monitoring the progress of students.

- Taking the register is an important part of the management of the school.

- The way you take the register helps to set the tone for the rest of the day.

2

Developing a Group Ethos

This is the most rewarding element of being a class tutor, but also the most difficult. Indeed, some would argue that it is not really necessary: as a tutor your job is to ensure that individual students are carefully monitored, allowing them to achieve the highest possible academic standards. Why do you need to cultivate a group ethos when, in many secondary schools, these students will not be taught together?

My response to that argument goes back to the issue of school ethos. If you value the individual student then it is important to offer them a sense of identity within a supportive group environment. Very often heads of year will organize competitions and activities, which will help to spark group interaction. House systems and competitions are part and parcel of some schools. Without this, however, tutors may want to try out some ideas. On induction day it is important to establish the idea that the tutor group is both secure and interesting. Activity 2.1 gives an example of an activity that will certainly encourage students to talk and interact. Tutees need to know each other's names just as much as you do and this offers an excellent mechanism for creating a group dynamic (although the pop group name will obviously need to be changed periodically!). In what is usually a welter of information about school uniform, planners and letters to be

13

Activity 2.1 Getting to know your tutor group

Read the list below. Move around the room asking people if they can sign against any of the things on your list. The only rule is that no one can sign your list more than once.

	Something about the person	Signature
1	They have an older brother at school	
2	They have an older sister at school	
3	They have a pet hamster	
4	They have been to Africa	
5	They were not born in England	
6	They own a Spice Girls CD	
7	They have been to Paris	
8	They have been to a wedding	
9	They have held a snake	
10	They have met someone famous	
11	They have flown in an airplane	
12	They have lied about their age	
13	They are frightened of spiders	
14	They have been fishing	
15	They have been on holiday to the USA	
16	They have a pet dog	
17	They are a member of a sporting club	
18	They have brown eyes	
19	They have paddled a canoe	
20	They have been to the cinema in the last month	

taken home, not to mention confusing tours of the school, this activity offers a quick way of establishing a positive feeling about the group for the start of the new year in September.

Another idea for the induction period is to set up a tacky postcard competition (see Activity 2.2). This is good fun, as well as giving you an early insight into the characters in your group. You probably will not get cards from every student, but those who send them will have already shown a sense of commitment and willingness to become involved. You will gain a sense of literacy skills, ideas about the things they enjoy doing, and the display will provide a focal point on the day of their arrival. Giving prizes for the card from furthest away, funniest, first to arrive, and so on, gives you a chance to shower the group with chocolate – bribery is, after all, one of the most effective ways of winning over young children (it may not be politically correct but it works!).

Activity 2.2 **Tacky postcard competition**

Send me the tackiest postcard you can find during the summer holiday. If you have time, tell me what you have been getting up to on holiday. Don't worry if you don't go away or visit anywhere exotic – I love getting postcards and will display your card with all the others in your tutor room ready for the start of the school year. Plenty of prizes – I look forward to seeing those cards!

Of course, there are problems with competitions. Often the same people win. One way around this is to create mini teams within the group. These can be the basis for competitions but can also be used as the focus for discussion groups when working through Personal, Social and Health programmes. The competitive urge is strong in most students and they enjoy the opportunity for collaboration and the sharing of ideas. This can also be linked into the development of literacy and numeracy – word games and number puzzles offer endless variations. See Activity 2.3 for some simple suggestions, but look on the Internet or in your local newsagent for puzzle books and activities. Make use of your Christmas games for ideas – Taboo, Balderdash, Trivial Pursuit, Scattegories, and so on.

Activity 2.3 Word games

- Girls names beginning with 'H' – 2 points for each name, 5 points if no one else has the name. 60 or 30 seconds for each round, teacher decision final. Countries, food, TV programmes, etc.

- As many three or more letter words as possible from 'registration'.

- Guess the teacher, figure from history, pop star *et al.*: name on sticker on back, only yes/no answers, swap questions with others in the tutor group. Tell the tutor when you've worked it out and then collect a new identity.

- Make up a mnemonic for a word which is difficult to spell – a prize for the funniest.

Competitions are by no means the only way of developing ethos. In my view the key to establishing group expectations is to get them to talk to each other. I know that this is 'more work and preparation' but in the long run it will make your own experience and that of your students much richer. See Chapter 3 on teaching personal and social education, which covers approaches to encouraging your tutor group to talk about serious issues.

Moving beyond the initial phase, it is important to get your tutor group to work together on specific targets. It is no good urging them to pull together just to 'feel better'. They need to know what's in it for them and they need also to see that there are specific, achievable targets. Look at the example in Activity 2.4. The targets are for a Year 11 class but they could equally apply to any year group. Notice that I have also set myself targets. The students need to know that you see the process of target setting as valuable and that you are prepared to stick your own neck out and make commitments. Subsequently the group can be divided into teams with responsibilities for particular targets. As they move through the school the group can become responsible for reviewing previous targets and setting new targets.

Activity 2.4 **Tutor group targets 2002–3**

◆ Target 1: To raise £250 for a charity.

◆ Target 2: To research up to five possible charities for the tutor group to support and present alternatives to group.

◆ Target 3: To organize a tutor group social activity for at least fifteen members of the group.

◆ Target 4: To ensure that the tutor group is involved in each inter-tutor group activity and to involve at least ten people in the teams.

- Target 5: To ensure that the tutor group is represented at year council, informed of decisions and discussion and also to make sure that the tutor routines run smoothly (e.g. register collected routinely, notices read and displayed).

Targets for tutor

- Target 1: To monitor the academic progress of students.

- Target 2: To ensure that all members of the tutor group receive relevant advice about courses for next year.

- Target 3: To ensure that the extended tutorial and citizenship programmes are relevant and taught appropriately.

The process of review and evaluation is vital if you are to ensure that the group dynamic remains appropriate. An evaluation sheet (see Activity 2.5) gives a chance for individual reflection before opening up discussion to the whole of the group. There is clearly a correlation between my targets and the targets for the group. I wanted to move them to a commitment to action rather than simply a nodding acceptance that 'all that stuff seems like a good idea'. As the principle of review and evaluation alongside target setting takes place you can also begin to challenge students to consider personal strengths, seek out opportunities for leadership or collaboration and tie in these qualities to their academic progress. Achieving targets can be rewarded collectively – thus avoiding the problems of the same students always winning the competitions. The question at the end of the tutor evaluation

'The students need to know that you see the process of target setting as valuable and that you are prepared to stick your own neck out and make commitments' is important. It makes the student think about why it is worth joining in the tutor group activities. When I asked my own group, they all agreed with the hypothesis that a clear focus at the beginning of the day set them up for the morning. The tutorial fulfils a similar role to breakfast!

Activity 2.5 Evaluation Sheet				
Name:				
Evaluation of tutor group:				

Statements	+ +	+	—	— —
I am happy in the tutor group.				
I see at least two other people in the tutor group socially, outside of school.				
I feel confident that I can contribute to discussions in tutor group time.				
The tutor group plays an important part in my school experience.				

Statements	+ +	+	–	– –
Things that we talk about in extended tutorial can be helpful.				
I think that I would talk to more members of the tutor group if we had to sit in different groups instead of with friends.				
I think that the tutor group could work better together if it was involved in more activities.				
I would be prepared to become more involved in tutor group activities if I thought other people were also going to make a commitment.				
Starting the day positively in tutor time would have a positive impact on my work in the first lessons.				
I want to help the tutor group achieve its targets for next year.				
I would be willing to help to raise £250 for a charity.				

I would be willing to help to research up to five possible charities for the tutor group to support, and present alternatives to the group.				
I would be willing to help to organize a tutor group social activity for at least fifteen members of the group.				
I would be willing to help to ensure that the tutor group is involved in each inter-tutor group activity and to involve at least ten people in the teams.				
I would be willing to help to ensure that the tutor group is represented at year council, informed of decisions and discussion and also to make sure that the tutor routines run smoothly (e.g. register collected routinely, notices read and displayed).				

On the other side of this sheet answer the following question: Do you think that the tutor group you are in can affect either in a positive or negative way the way you perform in your academic subjects?

Summary

- A group ethos is important and can be shaped.

- Establishing a group ethos is vital at the start of your relationship with your tutor group.

- The tutor group need to be involved in the process of shaping the group – not the victims of clumsy social engineering.

3

Teaching Personal and Social Education

Some teachers question whether or not tutors should deliver the personal, social and health education (PSHE) curriculum. Certainly many schools now deliver all or part of their programmes through specialist teams. The fact is, however, that many tutors will be expected to tackle some or all of a PSHE programme, including sex education, relationships, work experience, citizenship, drugs and health. For many teachers this is a daunting prospect, and they do not feel in any way prepared. Indeed, one of the main arguments against the delivery of PSHE by non-specialists is that they lack the necessary knowledge to inform and support the students in their tutor group. There are certainly training issues which have to be dealt with by schools who choose the non-specialist route. But this is not the place for such a discussion. If you have to do it then you need to think about how.

My view is that the role of the tutor in these situations is not to act as the expert who knows all the answers. It is far better to invite the school nurse, local vicar or community drugs officer to talk to your group. Indeed, if that is not already part of the school programme then why not suggest that your tutor group makes contact and arranges for someone to come in to discuss key issues? It is likely to be both informative and offer the students a sense of ownership of a programme which they often sense is being done 'to them' rather than 'for them.' In this way you will also be creating a link with groups within the community, which is part of the requirement for citizenship. You may feel more comfortable making the first contact, but students can be involved in the process of meeting the visitor, making them coffee before the tutorial, organizing the room and, most critically, asking the questions that they feel are important. Local groups from Amnesty International, local hospices, Oxfam, and a host of other charities and pressure groups will be only too delighted to come and talk. In this way the tutor can then take on the role of 'catalyst' without feeling that they have to offer expertise.

Perhaps the key role, therefore is, to promote discussion, to listen to views and help members of the tutor group reach informed judgements about the issues that are central to their lives. It seems so easy when you write it down but it is not so easy to initiate and manage group discussions. Getting children to talk is a specialist skill in itself that some teachers do not feel able to achieve, especially outside of the context of their specialist subject. My view is that the leading of discussion is a skill that can be developed. While nothing I'm suggesting here is new or revolutionary, it does work. As long as you make sure that clear ground rules are followed then most students will respond positively, especially if you have convinced them that the topic they are to discuss is worth their time and energy. The setting of the ground rules is something the group should also be responsible for – they can be printed and displayed so that transgressors can be picked up by their tutor or, more helpfully, by their peers. Indeed, the setting of the ground rules creates an opportunity for developing the skills essential for discussing key issues within PSHE. As with most of the ideas I'm going to suggest you should start with the individual. Ask the students to write down three rules about class discussion. Next get them to pair up and compare their suggestions. By doing this each person in the tutor group will have to talk (counting how many people have contributed to the 'talk' is important; if it is only two or three out of 25 then it's not working).

Once the pairs have talked you can extend the groups to four, this time asking the bigger group to define, within their collective list, the three most important rules. This will make the students refine and modify their own ideas in the light of the views of others. It will also require them to adapt and revise their written expression. All of this is music to the ears of your literacy coordinator and will also provide a foundation for academic work outside the tutor group.

Finally, you can move to the whole class discussion of the ground rules for tutor group discussion. It is here that some tutors would have started. They would probably report to their head of year or PSHE coordinator that their group was unresponsive, that they had no good ideas or that they had finished the task very quickly. Probably the tutor would admit to having written the rules up on the blackboard beforehand and then asked the tutor group if anyone disagreed! In that situation most young people will keep quiet. Who is going to stick their neck out and admit to the need to listen to the teacher? How many of the group will feel that there is a point to initiating the discussion if the rules are already decided? However, with the steady building and coalescence of ideas the students increasingly establish a sense of ownership. They want their ideas to be considered. They feel they have a chance of being heard within the whole class. More importantly, they have had a chance to develop their ideas so that they can rehearse some of the things they could put forward. This idea of rehearsal is vital: it helps to build confidence and ensures that students are not exposed to the embarrassment of saying something stupid.

I have included some examples of the ground rules that my tutor group worked out, but which do not represent a comprehensive list (Activity 3.1).

Activity 3.1   Ground rules for discussion in tutor time

- Only one person should speak.

- People should listen and not talk while someone else is making a point.

- No one should make fun of other people when they are answering a question.

- You can disagree with other people as long as you give your reasons.

- Respect the views of everyone in the class even if you don't agree with them.

- Don't use racist or sexist language or other language that will offend or upset other people in the group.

Once you have established the ground rules you also need to establish different types of talking situations. It is important that the group recognize that paired or small group discussion is as valid as whole class activities. As I have already described, paired and small group work can ensure that the 'talk' within the tutorial is extensive, inclusive and collect-ive. Students also need to recognize that their ground rules apply equally to small groups as to when the whole group is together.

Tutors may worry that students spend too much time 'off task' within these small groups. They are not controlling the discussion so how can they be sure that they are actually talking about the right things? This is a valid concern but should not cause you to abandon the approach. Liberated from the front of the classroom you are now in a position to 'cruise' – sit back and listen to a group's discussion or intervene to refocus discussion. We never worry, within the context of a large group discussion, about how many of our tutor group are actually thinking about the discussion. We might be disappointed if we found out! I recall a particular occasion when I was holding forth on a matter of great social significance – I think it was the death penalty – and one usually unresponsive student put up her hand. I was delighted that my rhetoric had challenged her. Imagine my despair when she said 'How much are flights to Ibiza at the moment sir?' I had always believed that while I was in control of the discussion everyone was on task when quite possibly half of them, or even more, were planning their holidays! Therefore, I think it is more likely that small groups of students will maintain a clear focus on a topic for longer. Also, the tutor is in a much better position to monitor their ideas because he or she can talk to students in small groups instead of fielding the thoughts of the articulate minority who tend to dominate whole class discussion.

In general terms I always feel it is best to avoid whole class discussions – these are difficult for groups of teachers to participate in and manage (think of your staff meetings), so why should young children be able to cope any better? Certainly I think whole class discussion should be the culmination of a process rather than the start. Imagine you are asked to lead a discussion with your tutor group on marriage and divorce. Give out the 'starter' activity (see Activity 3.2) and ask the students to complete it. Remind them that there are no right and wrong answers – this is about their own opinions. Next, ask the students to compare their opinions in pairs and identify one statement where they disagree strongly. Ask them to listen to each other's arguments. The next stage could then be to join with another pair to form four. Each person should then attempt to explain the arguments put forward by their original partner. As a plenary, one person in each four could be asked to summarize the issues discussed.

This approach to building a discussion works well. It also ensures that lots of students are talking – you can pretty well guarantee that everyone has contributed to the discussion, whereas in a whole class discussion the talking is often dominated by a few students. Moreover, it avoids putting students on the spot with difficult questions – 'What do you think about marriage and divorce Jenny?' Furthermore, it gives the students the opportunity to select the particular

Activity 3.2 Marriage and divorce

Statements	+ +	+	−	− −
Marriage is no longer necessary in modern society.				
Teenage marriage will always end in divorce.				
Marriage is best in a religious building.				
Divorced couples should not be allowed to get married in a church.				
People who live together should get married before they have children.				
Sex before marriage is okay.				
Sex is more important than friendship in a married relationship.				
If divorces were harder to get then more people would work harder at their marriages.				
It is better to 'stay together for the sake of the children' than put them through the trauma of a divorce.				

'Whole class
discussion should be
the culmination of a
process rather than
the start'

element of the question they want to discuss. It also makes them listen to the views of their partner so that they can repeat it clearly when the pairs join together. This approach can be used for any topic – and the starter activity can be varied.

Another approach to setting up discussion, and one which might be most commonly associated with primary schools, is 'circle time'. Sitting students in a 'round' and removing physical barriers is, however, a superb way of promoting and developing whole group discussion in a non-threatening way. Creating the circle in the first place requires strong elements of teamwork and collaboration. Once the circle is complete, and includes the tutor, who has now been removed from the 'front', eye-contact can be guaranteed and the discussion can begin.

You can experiment within the circle: the only person allowed to speak must be holding the board rubber, soft toy, etc.; you must sit alternate boy/girl – apply whatever rules you like. I use the circle as a way of discussing big issues. Typically I will raise an issue – for example, 'The age for legally drinking alcohol in pubs should be lowered from 18 to 16' – and then require each member of the circle to respond to the statement with a justification. I will insist that there are no interruptions or challenges and run through the group quickly. Next time around I will insist that they start by saying 'I disagree with X because ...' or 'I support the views of Y ...'. This encourages the students to regard the discussion as inclusive and linked together instead of providing a platform for their own point of view.

The circle can also be used for issues beyond the

PSHE programme. It offers an opportunity for airing views on school issues, evaluating the progress of the group and raising issues of concern over behaviour within the group. Because clear rules are applied and no one can 'hide', students will often speak openly. Naturally, the ground rules for discussion must also still apply.

The circle can also be flexible. I have used it as a starting point for role-play. Once in a circle the group receives a 'situation' (see Activity 3.3). Next, divide the group into smaller groups of three students, and have one of the three turn their back on the centre of the circle and face the other two 'knee-to-knee'. Two of the group then act out the scenario whilst the third observes, ready to report back at the end of the role-play. The resultant noise and frantic argument often seems chaotic, but it works – especially if you are prepared to give your tutor group plenty of practice. The key is to set it up clearly at the outset. Make sure that the groups have decided who is to observe, that the scenario is clear, and that pairs or fours have worked out adaptations for the observation/role play.

Activity 3.3 **Parents and teenagers**

Scenario 1

Teenager wants to go out, midweek, with friends. Parent wants teenager to do homework. Neither is willing to give in.

Observer should look out for the arguments used by both sides to justify their point of view and be ready to explain to the rest of the class what happened in the role play.

Scenario 2

Teenager's room is messy. Parent wants teenager to tidy up. Teenager wants to watch programme on TV.

Observer should look out for the arguments used by both sides to justify their point of view and be ready to explain to the rest of the class what happened in the role play.

Scenario 3

Teenager wants to go to party and stay overnight. Parent is worried about the possibility of excessive drinking and also child becoming sexually active.

Observer should look out for the arguments used by both sides to justify their point of view and be ready to explain to the rest of the class what happened in the role play.

Scenario 4

Teenager wants to get a part-time job in a local pub on Saturday night. Parent is worried about the late nights and the rough clientele.

Observer should look out for the arguments used by both sides to justify their point of view and be ready to explain to the rest of the class what happened in the role play.

After the role-play work out key points to advise both parents and teenagers on how to make their relationship work. This could be in the form of letters to an Agony Column or posters to be displayed in the classroom. This activity could be followed up by inviting some parents of children (maybe in the tutor group) to come in to discuss the problems of dealing with teenagers.

My experience of 'circle time' suggests that students feel more secure and are able to discuss sensitive issues in a way they might find impossible in a normal arrangement of desks and chairs. This view was confirmed when I was discussing the issue of death with a group of Year 11 students. I asked each person to talk about anything connected to the subject, but emphasized that they could choose to opt out as this was such a sensitive subject. I was surprised that most students chose to contribute. After the discussion had jumped from life after death, to euthanasia, to the death of a pet and back again we arrived at Nicola's turn. She paused, and then asked 'Can you see the flames when a body is cremated?' Alison, who had talked about her gran's cremation offered a description and reassured Nicola. I then asked Nicola if there was a reason for her question and she explained that her father had died when she was only four years old. Her mother had said that she was too young to attend the ceremony but this question had troubled her ever since. She hadn't wanted to worry her mother and this seemed like a good opportunity to find out.

Sometimes the responses can surprise you. In a citizenship lesson I was discussing in the circle whether violence was ever a way of achieving positive changes in society. Our discussion had ranged over fox hunting, the IRA and UN involvement in Iraq. When it came to Alan he paused and rocked forward saying 'I don't really know if violence works'. I thought this was a prelude to passing up his chance to speak and I was just about to move on when he continued – 'When I was at middle school I was bullied. The older boys would hold me up against a wall and punch me. My dad said I should hit them back, so the next time I did and then ran to the headmistress ... she suspended me' (gasps of indignation from the class who were hooked on the story) '... but she expelled the three kids who were bullying me!' (cheers from the circle). 'So I'm not sure if violence works or not.' Alan had held the group with his story. He had made a very important point, which demonstrated that there are few clear-cut answers when dealing with political, moral or social issues. Beyond citizenship, however, Alan had enjoyed an opportunity to display trust within the tutor group and confront openly issues of bullying that may well have been troubling other students within the group. I'd like to think it was my skills as a tutor which led to all of this crucial learning. All I can claim, however, is that I created a context in which Alan felt confident and where he was able to say what he needed to say.

Along similar lines students can be 'hot-seated'. One student can take on the role of a particular person (maybe outlined on a briefing sheet or based on a character from a TV programme, film, etc.) and they have to attempt to answer questions posed by the rest of the group. This allows individuals with talents to shine within the group and also can lead to penetrative thinking about key issues and questions which probe motives, personality and thoughts. Within the context of a PSHE course it is always possible to link into current moral and social issues through soap operas like *Eastenders*, *Hollyoaks* and *Coronation Street*. The plight of battered wives, the position of teenage mothers, the problems of sexually transmitted diseases, homelessness, and so on, frequently form the focus of storylines and students will be able to relate to these characters, often better than to stories from news bulletins, which they only rarely watch. A student hot-seating as Little Mo from *Eastenders* may well articulate emotions and views about battered wives that a theoretical discussion would miss. Even without the soaps, local papers will often provide a context for character exploration. You could choose to use the whole class as a forum for the discussion or build up with pairs and threes so that the 'performers' are less exposed, but whose views can then be shared with the whole class.

The methods of promoting discussion so far have been characterized by informality alongside clearly laid-out boundaries. Once the tutor group becomes confident with the application of rules they may welcome the opportunity for formal debate. Here the application of rules is important, but there is an additional sense of importance created by the formality of the situation. There is also an opportunity for you to work with individuals – your proposer, opposer and seconders – in advance to help them shape arguments. The responsibility for chairing the debate can be assumed by a member of the tutor group. This approach to discussion emphasizes discipline and self-control, and the formal nature of the debate requires some preparation. You have the chance to spend time with the speakers, helping them to build up their arguments. This further helps to cement your relationship with students individually. It also ensures that the debate has pace because the students have planned and rehearsed their ideas.

Summary

- The teacher should never pretend to be an expert.
- The key to effective PSHE is good discussion.
- Discussion-based work needs clear ground rules.

4

Teaching Citizenship

Citizenship adds to the challenge of the tutor. Politics is not the most obvious topic to excite young people and many share their parents' disillusionment with the political process. Calling the subject citizenship cannot hide the fact that tutors are being asked to establish and develop political awareness.

As with PSHE, the models for the delivery of citizenship will vary from school to school. Specialist teams, day conferences and cross-curricular entitlement programmes will have been developed. Alongside these models some schools will ask the tutor to deliver all or part of the citizenship programme. Just as in the PSHE course the tutor should not view him or herself as an expert. A shared exploration of issues helps students to understand that citizenship is not a defined body of knowledge that has to be learned, but is about developing values, an approach to political issues whereby the student can form their own reasoned judgements. Sometimes it is hard for politically active and aware tutors when they see their tutees developing lines of thinking that are not a reflection of their own. Sometimes you will hear the attitudes and prejudices of the parents being expressed by their children, with little personal awareness of the issues. Sometimes you simply have to bite your tongue; students must have the opportunity to express views and question accepted judgements. If they are not allowed to do this then we have arrived at the edge of a totalitarian system that directs the views of citizens. However, I do not believe that the tutor should never express views. In fact, I think it is vital that the tutor does express views, thereby offering a role model for his or her tutees. The key is to ensure that the views are clearly expressed as an opinion and that they are subject to challenge and questioning by the tutor group. Some teachers think that citizenship represents a minefield into which they are unwilling to enter; my view is that teachers must either accept the challenge of citizenship or face the consequences of political apathy in future generations.

I want to include two examples of ways to introduce the ideas of citizenship. They offer examples of approaches to citizenship and also slightly different approaches to developing discussion.

Activity 4.1 raises the key issues of citizenship. Students individually, then in pairs and groups, can be asked to award these three citizens marks out of 10, where 10 is a good citizen and 0 should see the character deported or imprisoned! The next challenge is for the groups to generate their own 'good citizen'. This can be a portrait in words, or groups could draw a 'stereotype'. With the concept of citizenship established as part of the students' understanding and some issues raised about the nature of 'good citizenship', other tutorials will be much easier.

Activity 4.2 extends the ideas of citizenship but allows the students to explore them within a fun context. My caricatures of leaders in the activity are based on teachers known to the students. I always

'My view is that teachers must either accept the challenge of citizenship or face the consequences of political apathy in future generations'

Activity 4.1   Good citizens?

Albert Smith

Albert Smith is 56 years old. He has lived in the same house, in the same town for the last 40 years. He has worked at a local factory, paying taxes and contributing to a pension scheme.

He has never voted in a general or council election. He doesn't trust politicians. He has saved up nearly £20,000 which he keeps in the bank. However, he would never give any money to charity. In fact he is often rude to people who come round to his house collecting; he says they are all scroungers and should look after themselves.

Vanessa Williams

Vanessa Williams is a single parent. She has three children all between the ages of 5 and 10. The children's father is a drug addict and has no contact now with Vanessa. She lives in a council flat and receives a number of benefits. She does not work and at the moment is quite happy to receive money from the state to look after her kids.

Vanessa's own drug habit is now under control but she attends a rehabilitation clinic once a month. Her probation officer is pleased with the progress she has made since receiving a community service order after she was caught shoplifting.

Vanessa regularly attends Gingerbread meetings (a group that helps single parents) and has recently agreed to help distribute the group's newsletter.

Alan Jones

Alan Jones is in a wheelchair as the result of a road accident. He was driving home from an office party when his car collided with another vehicle. When police breathalysed him he was over the limit and was convicted of drunk driving. The judge decided that he should not go to prison in the light of his injuries but he had to pay a large fine. The death of the driver in the other car plays constantly on his mind.

Alan had run a small company employing eight other people but the business collapsed after his accident and police charges. He has not been able to find work since, although he has attended the local college, completing a number of ICT courses. He enjoys meeting other people and, because of his disability, he doesn't have to pay.

Since being in a wheelchair Alan has worked voluntarily for the Headway charity which raises money for people who have suffered head injuries in road accidents.

Discussion points

♦ What makes a good citizen?

♦ Make up a profile of someone who is a 'good citizen'.

♦ What qualities should they have?

♦ What should they do?

♦ Should we have to prove that we are good citizens before we can receive benefits?

think that if you can make the student laugh then they will not notice the 'learning medicine' go down. By using recognizable characters they also begin to realize that they exist within a 'political' community with its own tensions so that they can increasingly relate to leadership struggles on the wider political stage. The *Lord of the Flies* model offers huge potential. Once you have dealt with the issues of leadership – perhaps with members of the tutor group role playing the key characters – you can conclude with a vote. The electoral process involves all students in the decision making process and models the political issues which you are required to teach. Furthermore, law making, sanctions, culture and identity, rights and responsibilities and many other key concepts present themselves for development.

Activity 4.2 Who should be our leader?

Stranded on a desert island you have to choose your leader. The following are the people who have put themselves forward.

Geoff Smith

Geoff is a fast runner, physically strong. He's good at every sport and he's also good with words. He's got very clear ideas about how to lead the group and he is determined that people will do exactly what he says.

Geoff doesn't like the idea of anyone challenging his leadership of the group. He's already had a number of arguments with people about how things should be done. As he is good with words he very often gets his own way.

Petra Watson

Petra is always smiling. She wants to include everyone in making decisions. Anything decided must be agreed by a majority of people – ideally everyone! Petra is not physically strong but she is good with words.

Petra is a good listener and tries to include everyone's views. This is sometimes really hard because different people want very different things.

Nai Putrats

Nai is from Eastern Europe. His English is a little difficult to understand but he is very enthusiastic. He has practical survival experience from when he lived in the mountains around his birthplace. He can build shelters and he is very strong – he is definitely not frightened of hard work.

Nai believes his understanding of the great outdoors would help him to make the best decisions for the group.

Dana Roe

Dana is a party girl. Everyone loves her and she loves to have a good time. She thinks everyone is taking this whole situation too seriously. She thinks Geoff is a control freak and that Petra will never get anything done.

Her idea for the group is that they should have fun: rescue is just around the corner – 'So why the long face?'

Much has been written recently about learning styles and there is a vogue for 'kinaesthetic' learning opportunities. In short, some students learn more effectively when encouraged to move around. There are ways of developing this within tutor time. Moreover, it can also promote different types of less formal talking.

Creating posters on a given theme may seem passé, but I feel it can genuinely motivate and engage the students. It will also give you an opportunity to experiment with groupings. The posters may be part of research on a particular theme – for example, the role of different pressure groups like Greenpeace, Friends of the Earth, Amnesty International, and so on. The production of the poster could form part of a presentation for the whole tutor group. This adds even more credence to the claim that tutor time is an ideal time to deliver not only the citizenship programme but also key elements of the literacy strategy. Dealing with the practicalities of who does which job is also a vital part of the bigger picture for citizenship. If you are worried that the poster will simply become an 'information dump' with huge sections copied from the Internet or publicity leaflets, you can set questions that require answers. For example, 'What are the main methods used by Greenpeace to put over their ideas?' or 'Would a vote for the Green Party be a wasted vote?'

Another idea is a line of continuum. Take a list of characters and give one to each student in the class. Ask them to arrange themselves into a 'Happy/Sad continuum' with the happiest on the right and the least happy on the left (Activity 4.3). Then suggest that they change the order so that the person with the most political power goes on the right and the least political power goes on the left. This works particularly well if you limit the numbers of characters to about twelve or thirteen – about half the class. Next, put two rows of chairs facing each other and get the students to arrange themselves. When they discover that the two groups have come up with different sequences this will provoke animated discussion, in this particular case focusing on where political power rests and whether political power brings with it happiness.

Activity 4.3 Happy or sad?

- The Prime Minister
- A High Court judge
- The editor of a national newspaper
- The owner of a cable TV company
- A teacher in a secondary school
- A nurse

◆ A fireman	◆ A checkout worker in Tesco
◆ A highly paid footballer	◆ The chief executive of a large supermarket chain
◆ A pop star	◆ A homeless person

As a result of placing themselves physically within a line and informally discussing with their peers the appropriate position for their character, every student has a sense of ownership in the activity. Once the line is established you should then ask the students to reveal their identities and explain why they have positioned themselves in a particular spot. The other line can challenge the decisions and put forward alternative reasoning. Often students who will not normally volunteer information are motivated to speak. Of course, there are no right answers here and students need to be encouraged to argue and experiment with ideas. If they become preoccupied with the need to second guess the teacher then the point of the activity is lost. If you want to turn the continuum into a competition then you can award points for the best arguments put forward.

This is by no means a comprehensive approach to making students talk. What it offers are starting points. By building confidence through exposure to different approaches to discussion you will find that the group creates its own momentum and PSHE becomes an integral part of what you talk about in tutor time.

Summary

- You need to create an environment where opinions can be shared and valued.

- Teaching citizenship matters, but the students will only value it if you do.

- Citizenship is not a body of knowledge but is about setting values and expectations.

5
Managing Difficult Students

The majority of the students in your tutor group will probably offer few challenges in terms of behaviour and their own personal problems. However, there will be occasions where you need to respond to students whose behaviour is inappropriate. Often this behaviour will manifest itself elsewhere in the school and may be connected to a whole range of circumstances outside of school. While accepting that students' bad behaviour is not 'their fault', your role as tutor is to explain why they must modify their actions.

While there is always a need to deal with individuals you should also take the opportunity of addressing the issue of behaviour with the whole tutor group. Within circle time you could discuss key issues about school:

♦ What makes for a good lesson?

♦ Why do some people behave inappropriately?

♦ How should you respond if someone is disrupting a class?

♦ Why do students disrupt some lessons?

The list could go on, and the discussion would highlight key issues for all students. Moreover, those in the group who are disruptive will be confronted, directly or indirectly, with the consequences of their behaviour. Naturally it is vital that all students are allowed to speak – both those who suffer the disruption to learning and those whose behaviour is inappropriate. In this way no one can feel that they are being criticized or ignored.

To develop this you can move into triplet role plays (as described in Chapter 3). Outline a number of scenarios in classes where the teacher is confronting bad behaviour (Activity 5.1). Allow the students to act out the dialogue and then review the process, with the observers reporting back on issues like body language, problem resolution, mistakes made by the 'teacher', and ways of compromising. This would be a superb activity for staff training – with students and teachers involved in role reversals so that everyone could see the issue of behaviour from different perspectives.

Activity 5.1   Students behaving badly

Scenario 1

Martin Muddle is in a science lesson, and the teacher is leading a demonstration prior to the students completing their own practical. The teacher is concerned that the students are aware of what needs to be done and, in particular, about their behaviour in the lab because they will be using some acids and Bunsen burners. Health and safety issues are paramount to the teacher's mind.

Martin Muddle is frequently in trouble in science. He often arrives without equipment and is put in detention for not completing homework. Students in the group know that he is easy to wind up. During this demonstration, unnoticed by the teacher, someone has thrown Martin's pencil case under the bench. Martin is agitated and, in trying to reclaim his property, he has pushed over another student, creating complete disruption to the demonstration.

Scenario 2

Cheryl Chatter never stops talking. Her topics of conversation revolve around boys, clothes, make-up and nights out. She is not, therefore, that bothered about the content of her class discussion for integrated humanities about Fair Trade and the need for moral trading policies in the Western world.

The teacher is keen for the whole class to listen to different points of view. She is also aware that the time for discussion is limited and that the topic will most likely comes up in the examination in a few weeks.

Cheryl is chatting to her friend Natalie – she is being very quiet (mostly) apart from occasional snorts of laughter, but there is a constant murmur while other students are expressing their opinions.

The teacher has warned Cheryl twice to stop, but she has continued to ignore her.

Scenario 3

Lucas Loudmouth is really hard to teach because he is constantly shouting out answers in class. He also tries to get away with wearing his trainers in every classroom, knowing that most teachers will shy away from confronting him because he always makes a scene. The maths class he is in is low ability and full of quite volatile students who get very excited when there is a row in class.

Lucas has arrived this morning with baseball hat and trainers. When challenged by the teacher he has removed his hat but not changed into his shoes. He is now sitting at his desk but the lesson has not started.

Tasks

♦ Act out the scenarios.

♦ Discuss the way the student and the teacher reacted in each case.

♦ Try to work out 'Five top tips for teachers handling students behaving badly'.

Once the students begin to explore these scenarios they will begin to understand the perspectives of their teachers and this may help them to modify their bad behaviour in class. As a tutor you can then refer back to the discussions during tutor time when dealing with individual instances. Encouraging the student to see situations from different perspectives is a vital first step in changing their behaviour.

There is something chilling about the phrase, called out across the staff room, 'Is Peter Wright in your tutor group?' There is a sense of guilt by association. You too are being accused of writing pornographic graffiti on the science bench, shouting out obscenities during silent reading, or failing to complete homework for the fifth time that term. In this particular incident, Peter has refused to work with another student; the teacher, Mr Smith, has insisted, and Peter has walked out of the room and wandered around the school, returning at the end of lesson to collect his bag. At this point he has argued with Mr Smith who has put him in detention saying that he will talk to you, the tutor.

There are two likely reactions, neither of which offers a good way forward. The first reaction is 'Right, I'm going to have a real go at him! He won't know what's hit him! There will be no more messing around, mark my words.' If carried out, this rhetoric will have a disastrous effect on Peter. Threatening behaviour is going to sour your relationship with him; he will come to see you as the enemy, another person 'out to get him'. He will never open up about anything and, most importantly, he will probably continue to find ways to disrupt so he can achieve the 'double whammy' of riling you as well as his teacher. The second likely reaction is denial: 'Pete's a good bloke! His family background is a bit dodgy. You must be doing something wrong, he's fine with me.' This kind of reaction is less common but very damaging. Supporting your tutee against all the odds is not a way forward; you will do little to help Peter change his behaviour and you will destroy any chance of an effective working relationship with a colleague. Peter will not know what he has done wrong and your colleague will regard you as patronizing and ignorant.

Peter needs to be dealt with but you need to know the full story before you can help him. Spend time listening to your colleague. If you have received a note about Peter's actions, find Mr Smith and talk to him, sympathize with him and try to help him to define the problem clearly. Then speak to Peter.

'I hear there have been one or two problems in French, Peter, can you tell me about it?' Immediately Peter is disarmed. Your calm tone and invitation to him to put his side of the story have probably begun to win him over. But make sure you do listen. Waiting a few minutes then launching an attack on Peter's behaviour will only serve to compound the problem. You must constantly model appropriate behaviour; a calm, reasoned manner is critical and it is the kind of response you want Peter to learn. Keep asking questions about the incident – 'So what did you do? What did you say?' Move Peter towards a considera- tion of his actions – 'Do you think you handled the situation correctly? 'Now you have had time to think, do you think you might have behaved differently?' 'What do you think you should do now?' All the time the options are there for Peter. He has not been driven into a corner, he is not standing accused of a heinous crime, he is simply and fairly being asked to give his side of the story and suggest ways forward.

The situation is made more complicated when you feel that your colleague has over-reacted, when they have not offered the model of reasonable behaviour. When Peter tells you that Mr Smith called him 'An idiot, a waster' and has said that he doesn't ever want to see him in his lessons again, how should you respond? This situation happens all too often, and you can understand how the frustrations of dealing with Peter have led his teacher to extremes. Unfortunately Peter is now asking you if you think that 'Smith' was right to say those things and he wants to know if you rate 'Smith' as a teacher. This is not the time to dismiss your colleague and win over Peter, even if you think that Mr Smith has totally over- stepped the mark. 'Do you understand why Mr Smith may have lost his temper, Peter?' 'How would you have reacted in that situation?' Try to move Peter back to thinking about what he needs to do and how he can rebuild the relationship with Mr Smith. Eventually, you will reach a situation where Peter is ready to face Mr Smith, but it can be a good idea to prepare the ground with your colleague – 'I've talked to Peter and he realizes he's in the wrong, he will apologize and do the detention. He thinks some of the things you said to him were a bit harsh.' At this point you want Mr Smith to say 'Yes, I did go over the top, I'll make sure that I put things right.' Sadly, this doesn't happen all the time, and it is here that as a tutor you encounter a problem with school culture. In schools were the culture is conciliatory and supportive this kind of patching-up of a broken relationship will be happening all the time. It will be seen as a sign of strength on the part of the teacher and the student if they are able to sort out their differences. Sometimes, where the school culture is 'predatory', this approach will not work. Changing the behaviour of Peter Wright is something, as a tutor, you can work on and have some success with. Changing Mr Smith and helping him to deal more effectively with students is not your job and is very difficult if the culture of the school supports his approach. Some schools provide student complaint forms where they can highlight situations where they feel they have been mistreated by a teacher. The accusations can then be investigated and dealt with; the head of year will sometimes talk to Mr Smith, at your request, to seek to resolve the situation. It is at this point that, as a tutor, you begin to wonder what you can do to help Peter if Mr Smith is not prepared to compromise.

However, the positive point of this case study is that, by modelling conciliatory behaviour, tutors can help their tutees deal with situations they face in their relationships with their teachers. Of course, it is not always as easy as that. Invariably the same student in your tutor group will be causing problems around the school. It will not be a matter of one note but six or seven, and these notes will appear every week, not just once in a while. Is there any hope for the repeat offender? Can the tutor make a difference? I believe that he or she can. However, it is not something to tackle on your own. It is vital that the approach to dealing with difficult students is consistent. Often the year head will deal with 'intractable' problems, but they are increasingly bogged down by paperwork and case conferences. The tutor can and should initiate action and, hopefully, year heads will encourage their team to deal with issues in their tutor group. Every school has its systems and structures for this and working within those structures is important. However, there are important principles that will apply whatever the detail.

First, as I have already discussed, the modelling of appropriate behaviour by the tutor is vital. Second, whatever strategy is being used to change the behaviour of your tutee – a report card, detention, a letter home, internal exclusion – he or she needs to understand what is happening and why. The tutor needs to take time to explain, hopefully ensuring that the student realizes that the 'punishment' is both justified and designed to help them to improve their behaviour. This sense that the tutee can improve is vital. If students see no point in their report card then they will not behave differently in their lessons; if they understand why they are on report then there is at least a chance that they will respond appropriately.

As a tutor you have to accept that you will not 'win' in every circumstance. Very often the bad behaviour that manifests itself in school is a product of circumstances outside of the school environment.

'As a tutor you have to accept that you will not "win" in every circumstance'

However, the job of the school is to create a separate culture, one with clear values and structures. Students with difficult home situations will often see school as a secure and positive environment, a contrast to their home. As tutor you need to ensure that you convey that message.

One of the big issues in terms of behaviour in schools is bullying. In your tutor group you will have victims and perpetrators. Both need your support. Often the tutor group is the focus for bullying – the establishment of a 'pecking order' is seen as important by students arriving in a school. Schools will have policies for dealing with bullying and it is important to use these. My view is that the bringing together of the two parties is vital in dealing with the issue. Getting the bully to realize the impact that they have had on their victim is usually the most effective way of dealing with the situation. Often the bully will say 'I was only having a joke!'; they do not realize that their words or their actions are causing sleeplessness, anxiety attacks, depression, and so on.

Using a 'minder' is a good idea. Pick someone – sometimes it is a good idea to select a potential bully – and ask them to look out for any bullying of another student. Make sure they understand that they should not intervene but just let you know immediately. This can be difficult if the minder is unwilling to 'grass up' a friend, and it depends on a school culture where bullying is openly disapproved of and where students know that bullying is dealt with fairly and openly. The 'minder' system works well in many situations, especially if the tutor judges the situation accurately. The victim feels that they have someone looking out for them and the 'minder' has a sense of responsibility and self worth.

Another effective approach is to use the whole tutor group as 'guardian angels'. For example, I once had a student who appeared to have 'bully me' tattooed across her forehead; within days of her arrival in the school she was looking depressed and colleagues were talking to me about problems with low-level name-calling and teasing. I sent my 'victim' to the year office with the register and spoke to the rest of the tutor group: 'Changing schools is difficult for all of you, but Sally is currently finding it very hard. Some of you are making it even harder with unkind comments. You should be looking out for everyone in the tutor group, not making fun of them. Let me know if you see anyone being unkind to Sally and I will deal with it. I will tell Sally exactly what I've said to you, but I'm sure she would prefer it if you didn't make a big fuss.' It worked. The group took this student to their hearts, her confidence grew rapidly and by the end of the first half term she was well established within the group and was also enjoying success in lessons. Taking students into your confidence might be risky, and needs to be handled sensitively. However, I firmly believe that it further demonstrates the way that we can model appropriate behaviour for our tutees and achieve a supportive environment which is conducive to a positive social environment and effective learning.

Another strategy in dealing with 'repeat offenders' is to help them set behavioural targets, and undertake to monitor and reward their progress. For students who consistently fail to complete homework, set a target of recording their work for a week and check it daily. Reward them at the end of the week and discuss whether or not it has helped them to then go on to complete their homework. For students whose behaviour in class is inappropriate, set up a report card for the subject where they know their behaviour is worst and one for the subject where they feel their behaviour is best. Challenge them to gain 'good' comments in all the lessons. By focusing on two subjects you reduce the pressure of 'unremitting' good behaviour and help them to concentrate on key times. Allowing them to choose one of the subjects empowers them and ensures that they have a sense of control in the process. Some teachers argue that the report card is a waste of time. Students improve temporarily and then revert to their previous behaviour when the 'heat is off'. This may well be the case. If the challenge for the student is to behave in a particular way for the duration of the report then it is only to be expected that they will revert to their previous forms of bad behaviour. However, the most important part of the process is the debriefing: 'How do you feel it went?' 'What did you do differently?' 'How about in the lessons where you had no report?' 'What should we do next week?'

Time and time again I come back to the point that you need to offer your difficult tutees time to reflect and opportunities to change their own behaviour at the same time as modelling appropriate behaviour. This is why the role of the tutor is vital. You are the person who encourages the student to reflect on their behaviour, not simply the one who challenges their bad behaviour. Although there are no guarantees that you will effect a permanent improvement in the behaviour of a student, it does at least allow the possibility that change can take place.

There are, of course, many difficult students who may be in your tutor group, where the issues extend way beyond your remit. Working with Connexions welfare officers, the police and social services is not the responsibility of the tutor. However, it is important that you know what is happening. Talk to your year head, make a point of reading student files and be aware of out of school circumstances. I think that it is important that we do not, as tutors, interfere with the work of support services, dabbling with amateur psychology and stumbling into situations with little more than good intentions. But being informed is important. If you can begin to understand the situations facing a member of your tutor group you can at least start to empathize and perhaps protect them within the day-to-day routines of school.

Summary

- As a tutor you must model good behaviour.

- Set and monitor targets for students.

- Work as a team with your colleagues.

6

Meeting the Needs of Different Year Groups

Different schools will have different ideas about the tutor's role. Some schools will set up specialist teams for particular year groups – once a Year 7 tutor always a Year 7 tutor. In other schools you will spend a longer period with a tutor group. Sometimes this will be two or three years, sometimes longer. This enables the tutor to develop a good relationship with their group and may promote a higher level of care. Whatever the system, there are times when specialist knowledge is important, in particular at points of decision within the students' education – arriving at a new school, Year 9 options, work experience, or preparing for work, further and higher education. There are also the times of annual review when the tutor report has to be written. These issues will be covered in this section. The same premise remains as in earlier chapters – as the tutor you are not the expert, but rather the 'informed friend', there to direct the student to information and expertise, and to be available to listen to their anxieties.

The creation of a group identity was dealt with in Chapter 2. This is all part of the process of helping students to cope with their new environment. In my first school I recall that within twenty minutes of my arrival seven of my new tutor group were in floods of tears. I had not raised my voice and had been nothing other than a model of calmness and moderation. What I hadn't considered was that most of the children I was talking to had come from primary schools with all-female staffs. My deep voice and physical presence had been sufficient to trigger mass hysteria! Opportunities to meet with new students and parents prior to the start of the new school year are important and will help to smooth the process of entry into a new school.

For those students arriving new into your tutor group from another school there is a need to consider how to ensure that they are accepted quickly. Simple things like arranging for the new arrival to shadow a member of your group while timetables and sets are organized are helpful. Providing the kind of induction material – school plan, behaviour code, timetable printout and so on – they will need to ensure that they are at least able to refer back to things after the first day at school. This may be enough; most young people are quick to form friendships. But to speed the process you could do a *This is Your Life* hot-seating interview with the new student, highlighting previous school experiences, interests, and so on.

Anxiety and uncertainty accompany any time of change in a child's education. Year 9 options are a good example. For the first time students are confronted by decisions which they believe may affect the rest of their lives. Clearly this is not likely to be the case but, nonetheless, the onset of panic caused by the sense of the imminence of adult decisions, when they really do not feel equipped, is one which the tutor can help to alleviate. Talking to the whole group to explain not only the structures and procedures but also the significance of choices is important. 'You will not be allowed to make choices which will damage your future ...', 'You will need a core of subjects which will ensure that you are able to continue with any career in the future' – these are the points of reassurance that will help students recognize that they are not about to forsake a career in films if they decide not to take drama.

The relationship between subjects and careers is something that young people do not fully understand. They equate the study of history, for example, with a job in museums, the study of geography with an intimate knowledge of maps, and so on. I remember one of my tutor group explaining their decision to study geography: 'I am going to be an electrician and so I need to study geography so that when I am driving around I can find the next job'! There are often genuine misunderstandings about subjects and courses that the tutor can put right. Often students will be unsure about vocational courses and their links with traditional academic subjects. Time spent looking together at course materials can ensure that students begin to make informed decisions rather than making options choices based on assumptions and the plans of their friends.

Perhaps one of the hardest issues to deal with is parental pressure. Clearly parents have a vested interest in ensuring that their children are prepared for the future, but this sometimes extends to insisting on making choices for their children. I have often listened to members of my tutor group sigh deeply and say 'My dad says I have to take business studies so that I will be able to get a better job; I'd much rather do art, but how will that help me in the future?' Of course, there are a number of ways of dealing with this. The coward will say 'Perhaps your dad is right, better do what he says'. Alternatively, the sneak will say 'Put down art anyway and if your dad notices say that business studies was full so you had to do art instead'. The letter or phone call that may follow this approach is not easy to deal with and the strategy not to be recommended!

My approach is to rehearse the arguments with the student. Explain that success at GCSE is most likely when students are interested and motivated. Point out that there are no jobs that require a qualification in business studies. Point out that there are a huge number of jobs in design, the media and so on that highly value a GCSE in art. In particular, point out that art requires extensive use of ICT, which will be vitally important in work. Often parents' ideas about 'good option choices' are based on a misunderstanding of the subjects available. 'It was never like this in my day' is often muttered by parents at open evenings, expressing both their bemusement and also envy at the opportunities now available to their own children. If the student is still feeling bullied then it might be appropriate to telephone the parent to explain your concerns.

You may think it is hardly worth the bother, but that is the point: taking an interest in this kind of thing is what makes the role of the tutor worthwhile and important. If your tutor group has completed all the paperwork on time, and that is all that matters, then your role is no more than an administrator. If, on the other hand, you want to ensure that your students are on the best courses for them, then you will want to spend time making sure that they are happy, worrying far less about the deadlines and the potential for parental hassle.

This situation is mirrored when students reach Year 11. Post sixteen options are far more complex. There is also an added element of pressure in that the school is always keen to keep students at school purely from a financial point of view – if they leave it may have an impact on staffing and group size. In addition, there are genuine choices at post 16. Even with the broadening post-16 curriculum, with only four subjects students may be making choices that will limit their careers opportunities. Equally they need to make decisions that reflect their academic potential. There are two main dangers that we face as tutors at this stage. First, we can become like parents, knowing what is best for our tutees. We must avoid at all costs making choices for our students. Second, we can offer advice born out of ignorance or prejudice: 'You don't want to do that course at college, it's rubbish!' is an unprofessional response and one that demonstrates lack of understanding about how to make decisions.

The critical role of the tutor at this stage is to ensure that students are informed, open-minded and willing to explore opportunities. Just because you want to teach a particular student next year in your subject area does not give you the right to exert your influence over a student's decision. A wider choice of vocational courses offered by colleges of further education may well suit

'The critical role of the tutor at this stage is to ensure that students are informed' more able students as well as those less likely to achieve five A–C passes at GCSE. Modern apprenticeships are another route, which will suit some students perfectly. Why not invite college course directors and former students, now on college courses, to talk to your group? Organize a tour of a local college. Make every effort to ensure that options are explored, modelled on the way you would select appropriate courses for yourself. Moreover, help students to recognize that decisions made in January and February are not binding. Many students feel that they are obliged to accept either college or school; they are concerned that accepting places on more than one course is inappropriate. Until they see their examination results in August they have every right to pursue any number of options and they should be encouraged to keep doors open, not closed. It is at this stage that I feel that the tutor can really play a significant role. Despite the best possible intentions of Connexions advisers, careers counsellors, and so on, there is no doubt that the tutor will know the student best and will be able to have sustained dialogue with him or her rather than a one-off 50-minute meeting.

One of the main issues to deal with is the fact that students feel increasingly aware of impending adulthood. They are worried about letting other people down and they are concerned about their own futures. This is not an easy time and reassurance that their feelings of uncertainty are entirely normal is incredibly helpful to students. Time and time again through this book I have emphasized the point that tutors are not experts, but they are able to provide an adult view and a listening ear while young people grapple with important issues in their lives.

Writing reports

While most of the tutor's role is informal and discursive, there is an important function in both formative and summative assessment. Apart from the student and the parent the tutor is likely to be the only person to read the complete report for any student. As the 'educational expert' it is your role to interpret and highlight key issues to ensure that the student can make progress. Within a space of three or four sentences you need to pinpoint key areas for development, highlight helpful strategies and offer praise for achievement. In Activity 6.1 I have included some sentence starters that may help to formulate ideas. I do feel that the tutor has a vital role in the reporting system. Increasingly reports are generated from statement banks, cut and pasted from one student to the next, and the tutor report represents the principal, personal comment in the document from an adult who knows the student and who has an interest in their progress.

Activity 6.1 **Some sentence starters for reports**

- Rachel has made significant progress this year, particularly in ...

- Eric needs to improve his personal organization; this was commented on by a number of teachers, especially in ...

- John is to be praised for his work in ...

- I am concerned about George's negative attitude, particularly in ...

- Aziz is good at discussion; this was commented on by a number of teachers ... and this is important because it shows ...

- I am delighted by Imran's attitude to work, especially in ...

- Beth should look for more opportunities to contribute in class discussion, especially in ...

- A number of teachers have expressed concern over Gina's attendance, she should try to do something about this ...

- Aaron should aim to include more detail in his written work, particularly in ...

- It is good to see that so many teachers have commented on how well Lizzie works in small groups ...

From these starters you can see how the tutor can highlight 'the bigger picture', encourage and exhort, and also begin to suggest targets and strategies for the next few months.

Increasingly, schools require students to set termly or annual targets. While these will need to meet the requirements of the individual student there are clearly generic statements that will help your tutees to identify appropriate personal targets. A sample of possible targets is laid out in Activity 6.2. These targets should be directly related to issues raised in the report and should meet the needs that the student themselves recognize. They should, ideally, be a combination of 'hard' and 'soft' targets – both measurable but also qualitative. These targets should be something that actually matters to the

Activity 6.2 Sample possible targets

- I will aim to improve my personal organization by recording homework in my work planner and showing it to my tutor every Monday morning.

- I will aim to improve my attendance in the next month. Last month I attended only 75 per cent of sessions and so in the next month I will aim for 90 per cent (54 sessions out of 60).

- I will try to improve my contribution in class discussion in English lessons, so that I can improve my speaking and listening mark.

- I will aim to improve my performance in mathematics by asking the teacher more questions instead of relying on my friends to explain after the lesson.

- I will try to make sure I complete homework more effectively by setting aside time working in my bedroom with the TV turned off.

- I will focus on the theory work in PE, because it is the part of the course I find most difficult and most boring. I will get my folder sorted out with dividers and a contents page.

- I will get up 30 minutes earlier on school days so that I can arrive at school on time. I want to make sure that I don't get one late mark in the next month.

- I will make sure that I start researching courses for next year so that I can make a good decision over my option choices.

student and around which can be built a dialogue which will enable them to focus on how they can improve their academic progress. The key element is dialogue; don't get bogged down in semantics but do make sure that the conversation you have with the student is relevant and not obscured by educational jargon. It is so easy for us to create a mystique about school by talking to students about 'performance indicators', 'personal target setting', and so on. What we must ensure is that students reflect on how they can develop.

Reflection is at the heart of self-improvement and represents one of the main goals for any tutor. Any student who is self-evaluative, thinks critically about their learning and is prepared to listen to advice on how to improve is a student who will succeed. This is where the tutor can make a significant contribution to the performance of the student in lessons and in public examinations. One of the main times for reflection comes at the end of Year 11, when students write their personal statement in the National Record of Achievement (NRA). Ironically, this is really too late. You need to develop a culture of self-assessment and reflection throughout your time with your tutor group. While the suggestions outlined below will help students to write their personal statement and also set targets for improvement in the future, there is no reason why they cannot be used throughout the student's time in the tutor group. As you can see, this table is far from complete. That is part of its function – to provoke you and your students to develop your and their own approaches and strategies.

Activity 6.3   Personal qualities: finding the evidence

Quality	Demonstrated in school	Demonstrated out of school
Reliability	Collected the register for the tutor group.	Arrived on time for my part-time job every day in the last six months.
Teamwork	Represented the tutor group at volley ball, we lost in the semi-final.	Part of a scout expedition to Derbyshire.
Imagination	Art portfolio work on a theme of 'Beginnings and Endings'.	
Patience		
Personal organization		
Communication		

Add in your own examples and extra qualities. Some examples have been included in this sheet to guide you.

Summary

- Listen to your students and understand their needs.

- Never try to tell students what to do – give them access to the information they need to make their own informed decisions.

- Be a 'critical friend' but be generous with praise.

7

Helping Children with Problems

There are no simple answers. Every student with a problem creates a unique set of circumstances for which you will have to decide upon the best response. In this section I will consider the tutor's response to death, divorce, drugs, pregnancy and depression. I am not an expert. But that is the point – as a tutor you are not the expert and it is important not to attempt to do the job of the experts. At the same time, it is you in front of a group or with an individual and you need to consider the best way to deal with situations that confront you.

The reaction of young people to death is impossible to predict. The death of a grandparent is in some ways the easiest situation to come to terms with. There is a sense of natural order. Unless the grandparent has been living with the family, the death is also distant. Perhaps more difficult is helping the child deal with the strains and pressures on their parents. An awareness of the situation, a willingness to ask how things are at home – this is nothing profound, but something that tutors are sometimes embarrassed to do. We forget that our tutees are just people and we need to reach out in a way we would hope our own colleagues might if we ourselves were facing similar circumstances.

The death of a parent is another matter. The circumstances will affect the situation – sudden loss or the culmination of a long illness will certainly affect the response of the young person. Either way, grief is not something that follows a pattern. Nor is there a gradual diminution as time passes; it is more like a roller-coaster with highs and lows, good days and bad days. When a child returns to school after a bereavement it is important that they feel they have somewhere to go so that they can be alone. They need to be reassured that their teachers know the situation and will understand if they need to leave the classroom. While the head of year may have arranged to inform staff it is your role to ensure that the student understands the arrangements. Counsellors say that it helps to mention the name of the person who has died. They also say that clichés and platitudes (while difficult to avoid) do not help. Talking is important and a way of dealing with grief. However, there is no point filling the conversation with loads of 'outside news'. Practical help is important. Look for ways you might help, for example by collecting work that needs to be caught up, or by seeing the examination officer to secure special consideration. While this may seem pretty meaningless and trivial, we have to accept that we cannot make our tutee feel better, but we can help them grow accustomed to their new situation. Simply by listening as they explain how they feel, describe the events of the funeral, or talk about whatever they want to talk about, we are offering them something important.

The death of a student in your tutor group is something even more profound and deeply shocking.

Helping Children with Problems

The natural order of life has been turned upside down. Furthermore, your tutor group is confronted with their own mortality in a very direct and frightening way. Thankfully this situation happens rarely, although its impact goes far beyond the tutor group. Schools that have had to deal with tragic accidents involving the deaths of students depend on experienced counsellors who know how to work with children and teachers, although the grieving will continue after they have left. As in all situations the tutor should offer a model for the behaviour of the students. Your grief will probably be as profound as that experienced by any member of your tutor group. You will want to share in their grieving, through attending the funeral with them, writing letters of condolence or reading prayers in assembly. However, I believe one of the key things is memorialization: the planting of a tree, the creation of a garden, or a plaque in a quiet area of the school. All this will help the students to remember and reflect, and it will allow the process of grieving to continue. There's nothing worse than ignoring the fact that someone has died – how does three weeks, three months or even three years make a difference? It is important that we help our students to confront death. Only then will they be able to come to terms with how they feel about the loss of a friend.

This sense of loss is something that children experience when their parents divorce. There are inevitably, in any tutor group, many students who have been through divorces in their families. The sharing out of their time and affection is part of a routine and it creates no significant problems. Someone told me of an overheard conversation between two boys who were describing their fathers: 'What's his name? Oh yeah, him! I had him once, he was okay!' There is certainly a sense in which family break-up and complex relationships are common-place. However, on the day that your parents announce that they are separating it does not help to know that loads of other people have had the same experience. This is happening to you and you have to deal with it. Moreover, these situations inevitably lead to a sense of guilt on the part of the child – they feel that they have done something wrong and have created the circumstances leading to the break-up of the family. The emotional problems generated by the divorce will have an impact on the student's work and while this may not seem the main issue at a time of family crisis, it is your job to monitor, support and report. Requests for information from colleagues will help you to identify problems emerging from the home situation. Talking to the student will help you to establish their sense of the issues and how their work is progressing.

Finally, you may want to talk to the parents. You may find it a little daunting to pick up the phone to discuss a child with a parent whose marriage is in crisis, but why? Their child's education is important and it cannot be ignored; parents need to face up to the facts that their personal problems will impact on their child's education and that they continue to be responsible for their child's progress at school. Talking to them helps and shows the student that you are willing to help them in practical ways to deal with the situation they are facing. As I mentioned previously, these parental contacts must be recorded and your head of year should be aware that you have talked to parents in this way.

Sometimes you may feel that a student tells you something that you must pass on. In particular they may reveal to you instances of physical, mental or sexual abuse. Clearly defined procedures will exist in your school, but not everyone will know what they are! Ask your head of year, who is the school's designated child protection officer. Make sure you record what you know and that you have passed on the information. This is a particularly difficult aspect of a tutor's role. Often you are passing on information that the student desperately wants to remain secret. However, you must not tackle these issues on your own; you run the risk of exposing yourself to public and legal criticism and you also place the child in increasing risk. The following four points appear on Teacher.net and offer very clear and helpful advice:

♦ Talk to the member of your school's pastoral team who has been designated as the receiver of information about possible/suspected abuse (whether it be physical, sexual or mental). Do this as soon as you suspect that a child may be suffering.

♦ Do not tell the child what you have done. This could severely compromise the trust you have built up.

♦ Keep a written record of who you have spoken to about any suspected abuse. Include details of what was said and when, and what was decided. Such records will be invaluable should you ever be asked to cooperate with any investigations that might take place.

♦   Store anything you commit to paper somewhere that cannot be accessed by any pupils or adults not directly involved in the matter.

Above all, never agree to 'keep a secret' or offer complete confidentiality to a child. It may well be essential for you to pass information on to other people for the child's safety and if they believed that you had given them your word not to tell anybody, trust would be destroyed.

The role of the tutor in this situation can be difficult. The student may want to ask you who is in the right and who is in the wrong. Sometimes it seems obvious! But our opinion will not help the student come to terms with the situation. Our willingness to listen, our interest in practical matters – who they will live with, when they will visit – are important. Equally important is ensuring that colleagues know – often parents will not inform the year head and the first information received in school is from the students themselves.

The striking thing about these situations is the resilience of children. Furthermore, they are incredibly quick to support each other; the support networks created by young people are often more effective and practical than those that exist to support their parents. I have often been informed by a member of my tutor group about one of their peer's problems with regard to divorcing parents, and then reassured that they have everything in hand, knowing exactly what is needed as they experienced a similar situation last year! As a tutor you can sometimes feel redundant,

'The support networks created by young people are often more effective and practical than those that exist to support their parents' but the fact is, no matter how concerned you feel, you are not their friend or confidante and nor should you be. This kind of support network operates more effectively without your interference and you should leave well alone.

This is often good advice as far as tutoring is concerned, but there are occasions where you have to weigh up your options and decide if you should intervene. What should you do if you know or suspect that members of your group are experimenting with drugs? The fact is that, in secondary schools, almost a third of your group will have used illegal drugs in the last year and approximately one in five will have used drugs in the last month. So what? In our liberal society personal choices and freedoms are much vaunted. Is it our job to decide what choices young people should make? I think the answer to that question is 'yes'. I cannot imagine how I would feel if I suspected that a member of my tutor group was experimenting with glue and aerosols, but said nothing, then to discover that they had died. It is an untenable thought. As tutors I believe we have a responsibility to challenge behaviour and actions that are a danger to the individual. But what is the right approach? This is more difficult to state. In an ideal world you should talk to the student and share your concerns: 'You seem to be behaving strangely Jon, is there anything wrong?' 'Are you taking any medicines that you haven't told me about?' The questioning should not be accusatory or condemnatory. You need to give them space and time to answer the questions, and choices about how they are to approach the conversation. If your suspicions are aroused by unusual behaviour at a lunchtime registration it is probably not sensible to broach the issue immediately. If they are behaving strangely they are not likely to be thinking straight. It may be best to delay the conversation until the morning, having spoken to colleagues who taught the student in the afternoon to establish whether or not they observed unusual behaviour.

Of course, this conversation may or may not have an obvious outcome. Even the thought that you are suspicious may lead the student to stop experimenting with substances, at least while at school. There is not necessarily going to be a tearful admission of 'wrong doing' followed by a desperate plea for rehabilitation: this is real life, not *Grange Hill*. You may never know if your quiet words played any part in helping the student to make appropriate decisions about their use of drugs. But if there is no further evidence of unusual behaviour then there is nothing more to do. However, a continuation of unusual behaviour – which could be anything that is different from normal, e.g. listlessness, agitation, aggression, etc. – cannot be ignored. It is at this point I would talk to the head of year and discuss options. Is this the right time to share your concerns with parents? Should another adult – the head of year or school counsellor – talk to the student? There is no right answer; the circumstances will dictate the most appropriate course of action. Ultimately, however, one should not ignore the rights of the parents to know of your concerns; this is certainly true when the behaviour of the student is having a detrimental effect on their learning. This is usually my own key indicator; we are required to ensure that students achieve their true potential at school and we must address, as far as possible, issues that may prevent that happening.

In approaching parents I do not think that a blunt statement, such as 'We think he's on something', is the right way forward! The parents should be invited in, with their child, to discuss their progress. This will give you an opportunity to explain your concerns openly in front of the parent and child. I think that it is vital that the student is present. Secrecy will add to their suspicion and paranoia. It also reduces the risk of misunderstanding and misrepresentation. It is always good to have both tutor and head of year present; this will help to ensure that a fair record of the discussion can be recorded for the file and allow time for considered points to be raised. It is vitally important to ensure that these meetings are not confrontations. Sometimes parents will react angrily, either directing their rage at their child or the teacher. Most probably this will be a reflection of their anxiety and feelings of inadequacy as parents. As with all these situations the tutor must model the calm and reasoned voice. Moreover, there need to be practical suggestions – links with outside agencies, continued monitoring within school and reports to parents.

The situation with regard to drug abuse is often characterized as a 'battle', which implies that there is an enemy to be fought. We have to remember that this 'enemy' is not the student; in reality the enemy is ignorance and, as tutors, we must ensure that our tutees are informed and able to discuss issues related to illegal drugs in an environment that is supportive, informative and values the views of young people. An environment that fosters effective and open relationships is one in which students can make informed and reasoned decisions. We then have to place our trust in our tutees to make the right decisions for them; we cannot live their lives and nor should we try to.

A similar ethos must pervade when dealing with sexual choices. Young people will have sex and some teenage girls will become pregnant. Our responsibility must be to ensure that young people know about contraception. Teenagers still believe the playground myths that you can avoid pregnancy if you have sex standing up, or that you cannot get pregnant on your first time. One school nurse told me that she spoke to a girl who believed the she wouldn't get pregnant if she put a fizzy drink in her vagina after sex. The only way to reduce the risk of teenage pregnancy is to inform young people about contraception and allow them the opportunity to discuss sexual issues openly. But even with all this in place in a school, a tutor is still likely to be faced at some point with a girl who fears she may be pregnant but simply doesn't know what to do.

For some students their relationship with their parents allows for openness, but where the young person is unable to approach her parents then the tutor is often high on the list of candidates for 'confession'. Your job is not to take on the responsibility of the parent; you should not be offering advice. My view is that the only course open to a tutor approached by a student who believes that she is pregnant is to ensure that she contacts her parents. But there are ways of helping, by listening, by reassuring, and offering to telephone parents and explain the situation. You cannot promise to do nothing. As with other contacts with parents it is important to inform your head of year about your intentions and to take advice on the approach to adopt. Never act in isolation as a tutor otherwise you will leave yourself open to accusations of impropriety.

Dealing with depression amongst your tutees is an increasing issue. The pressures on teenagers appear far greater now than twenty years ago. In particular the pressures of examinations, the increased levels of expectation and pressure from teachers keen to 'enhance their stats' add to the conditions leading to depression. 'The Prozac Generation' might seem a rather melodramatic name but my experience suggests that the issue is real. In the USA schools have begun to screen all their students for depression in an attempt to reduce teenage suicides. Research suggests that up to 15 per cent of children are experiencing clinical depression. Indeed, the research highlights children as young as 7 experiencing the symptoms of depression. Is there anything the tutor can do?

In a sense the only thing that a tutor can do is what has been reiterated time and again in this chapter. If you have fostered an open and caring environment in which young people are willing to discuss ideas and share their views then you are more likely to be able to help those experiencing depression. If a young person feels isolated and lacks self-worth then they are more likely to become depressed. You cannot affect the circumstances outside of school, but within the school you can seek to ensure that students can access support and know that their views will be valued.

Summary

- The main thing you can do is listen.
- Do not pretend to be an expert.
- Never act in isolation.

Final Thoughts

As I write these final thoughts and reflect on the ideas I have written about I have the words of a colleague ringing in my ears: 'Do we really need tutors? Let's register them and get on with the business of teaching. It would be so much simpler and the kids wouldn't suffer.' Is that true? Have all the words I've written been a total waste of time? Just like the hours I've spent talking to, listening to, feeling frustrated by and agonizing over my tutor groups – all wasted? But the answer is no. There is some truth in the idea that we waste a huge amount of time on trivia. Our inefficient and needless administration eats up valuable time. And yet, the role of the tutor is at the heart of any good school because it is rooted in the building of relationships. These relationships will be the basis of the future success of the student in the school, of their ability to fulfil their potential. I do believe that schools can make a vital difference to the lives of young people and that tutors are at the cutting edge of that process. While some students will arrive in your tutor room with problems that will distract them from learning, in your role as tutor you are able to create a new situation with a clearly defined set of values in which any young person can feel secure and therefore able to move forward.

Summary: Top tips for the tutor

- Talk to your tutees.

- Set clear and high expectations.

- Form relationships.

- Ensure that administration supports rather than dictates your role.

- Believe that you can make a difference.

References

Audit Commission (2002) Introduction to website, *www.audit-commission.gov.uk/itc/attendance.html*

Ofsted (2001) 'Improving Attendance and Behaviour in Secondary Schools. A Summary of the Main Findings and Recommendations'. Ofsted Report HMI 242, February.

Tomlinson, M. (2002) *Annual Report from Her Majesty's Chief Inspector of Schools*. London: HMSO.